KEEP MOVING FORWARD

Not being moved by circumstance

———————

(Maribel Cota)

KEEP MOVING FORWARD

KEEP MOVING FORWARD
Copyright © 2019 by Maribel Cota

Fb: The righteous view
Instagram: The_righteous View
Instagram: mari_8081

ISBN (9781097360338)

KEEP MOVING FORWARD

Dedication

This book is dedicated to my late husband, Pastor Robert R. Hernandez, who died of cancer. You were an amazing man full of visions and dreams you will forever be in my heart. Also, to my late son, David A. Bernal, who passed away in a car accident; you never cared what people said about you, that was my favorite quality about you son. Also, to my daughter Kristie who is strong, courageous, and smart; I love you, never give up on your dreams. To my daughter Precious, who is creative and witty. Never allow your focus to move you away from your desires. To my son Robert, who is the "spitting" image of his father, caring and full of wisdom; may God's favor follow you wherever you go. And to my daughter Emerald Rose, funny and full of God-given talent; never underestimate the power that is within you. I also want to thank my parents Alberto and Maria Cota for never losing hope in me, for always being there, and praying for me in the midnight hours; even though we've been through 'hell' together, you both have shown me that with God, all things are possible. And most of all I would like to dedicate this book to my friend who never has left me nor forsaken me the one who has given me courage and a new life my Savior Jesus Christ. Thank you for everything you have done for me, Love you.

3

KEEP MOVING FORWARD

Table of Contents

KEEP MOVING FORWARD

KEEP MOVING FORWARD

Introduction

This devotional book has been in my heart since 2017, and through the grace of God it is finally here. During the writing of this book I was in a dark place in my life where God was showing me how to continue to move forward regardless of how I felt, what I saw, or what I heard.

I am definitely in a much better place now, and have overcome my struggles. I know God is not finished with me yet, But I am definitely "Moving Forward."

I pray these devotionals bless you as much as they have blessed me. Stay focused and alert so you can walk through your destiny with purpose and power.

You don't want to just be EXISTING in life, but you want to be LIVING in your full potential.

Be sober; be vigilant; because your adversary the devil walks around as a roaring lion, seeking whom he may devour. 1 Peter 5:8

KEEP MOVING FORWARD

The Lord GOD hath given me the tongue of the learned, that I should know how to speak a word in season to *him that is* weary: he wakeneth morning by morning, he wakeneth mine ear to hear as the learned.

Isaiah 50:4

KEEP MOVING FORWARD

Obedience is better than sacrifice

Day 1
Scripture: Deuteronomy 14:2 you have been set apart as holy to the LORD your God, and He has chosen you from all the nations of the earth to be His own special treasure.

When we hear God wants us to separate ourselves unto Him, we get very excited to know God has called us for a reason and a purpose. We start off right, reading His word and praying. Then as time goes by, we start getting distracted with the affairs of life.

The Israelites kept going around the same mountain because they had issues inside of them that God wanted to remove in their lives and break some cycles they had picked up from the Egyptians. God wanted to teach them His ways and His thoughts. So, when the pressures of life came their way, they would be able to endure and remain strong.

Do not be like the Israelites and not take heed to God's structure for your life, you never want to move ahead of God. You want to be in His perfect will. Stop and get into His presence and ask God to show you, if you have moved ahead of Him if you are in His perfect will or are you going solo in your journey. God will always show you where you need to be.

Make sure you start off at the right place - whether it is at the right church, in the right relationship, or at the right job.

Be obedient to where God is calling you and I assure you the blessings and the spoils will follow you in due season.

KEEP MOVING FORWARD

NOTES: DATE:

9

He is all mighty & powerful

Day 2
Scripture: Revelation 1:8 "I am the Alpha and the Omega," says the Lord God, "who is, and who was, and who is to come, the Almighty.

The words Alpha and Omega means He is the beginning and the end. We seem to forget at times that God created the universe and everything in it, we forget that everything is and will be because of His Mighty power.

Maybe because at one time or another you have asked for things and they have remained unanswered prayers. You forget at times that God is all powerful full of splendor (Magnificent) in all His wonder. He can create anything at the sound of his voice and destroy this whole universe if He wanted to.

That's the God you serve all Mighty and powerful, you are privileged to call him your Father, your friend, and you're Healer.

Walk around today with boldness and confidence knowing that your father is God almighty. He covers you with his presence, guiding you and protecting you.

The word of God says He goes before you preparing a way where there is no way, I say today BELIEVE, HOPE, and EXPECT great things from your father.

For He can and will answer your prayers maybe not today and maybe not tomorrow BUT the Lord does hear you and is well able to open the windows of heaven and pour out blessings that you will not be able to contain.

NOTES: DATE:

_____

_____

_____

_____

_____

_____

_____

_____

_____

_____

_____

KEEP MOVING FORWARD

What really matters?

Day 3
Scripture: Mark 8:36 for what shall it profit a man, if he shall gain the whole world, and lose his own soul?

In this world you hear at a very young age that you need go to college, get a degree so you can become successful and be well off. But in the end, none of that will matter, I'm not saying it's a waste of time. Because of course you will need to work to eat.

But what I am saying is there needs to be a balance. A balance will keep you focused on the things that really matter in life. Some people focus all their time and energy on losing weight, others on partying and meeting new people, some like to gear all their energy on what they love to do, playing music, watch sports, go golfing. None of those things are bad, but it becomes bad when all your time and energy is channeled to that one thing.

People began to worship these things in their heart and that's when it will start taking form of an idol. It will take all their heart, soul, and mind and before they know it, what really matters gets lost their daily activities.

Exodus 20:5 Thou shalt not bow down to any graven images or idols. God is not going to ask about how successful you become in life, But he is going to ask the question, "WHAT DID YOU DO WITH MY SON JESUS" did you feed the poor, and pray for the sick?

Did you show people there is a better life in Christ? Those are the questions, you will have to answer.

Today search your heart and get your focus back!!

KEEP MOVING FORWARD

NOTES: DATE:

Push through the crowd

Day 4

Scripture: Mark 5:27, 28. When she heard about Jesus, she came up behind him in the crowd and touched his cloak, because she thought, "If I just touch his clothes, I will be healed.

Push through the circumstances, push through the attacks of the enemy, push through the negativity and push through the fiery darts.

You are defeated because you sit back and allow the enemy to bombard you with nonsense. You sit back and feel like there's nothing you can do. But my friend you are defeated because you don't push through, God's word says "RESIST" the devil and he will flee. Another word for resist is to withstand.

The origin for with-is (against) so... That means to "STAND AGAINST" the enemy. It doesn't mean to sit or lay in your defeat. You need to PUSH THROUGH your circumstances, you need to get the little bit of energy you have left and claim your victory.

Speak with confidence knowing that God is on your side and the enemy is the defeated foe. (Opponent)

Today my friend shake off what the enemy is throwing your way and stop walking around with your head down, lift your head high, and say God "you're on my side" I walk in the victory you have died for me to have. I claim my blessings, I claim my financial breakthrough, I claim my healing, I claim the salvation of my unsaved loved ones, I claim my purpose coming to pass, I claim my VICTORY in Jesus Name. Today ...... I PUSH THROUGH!!

KEEP MOVING FORWARD

NOTES: DATE:

_____

_____

_____

_____

_____

_____

_____

_____

_____

_____

_____

Unity in the body

Day 5

Scripture: Colossians 3:15. "The peace of Christ rule in your hearts, since as members of one body you were called to peace. And be thankful.

It just blows my mind sometimes when I hear people say negative things about other churches; I'm talking about how I've even heard Pastors say not to go visit certain preachers.

Aren't we one body, One Church? I'm not talking about how we can just go anywhere to visit either because I know we need to be careful of who speaks into our lives, not everyone believes and teaches the same. But speaking of other churches and sowing negative seeds of other churches is not good, it brings strife amongst the body and that's exactly what the enemy loves to do.

In Matthew 12:25 "Every kingdom divided against itself will be ruined, and every city or household divided against itself will not stand. The enemy knows that we become weak when we are divided, so his aim is to get the body against itself.

As Christians we are to have nothing to do with strife because it's always caused by ungodly traits and it leads to arguments. It is caused by things that have no business in Christianity like pride, hate, and jealousy. We are to love others as ourselves, but strife does not do that.

Proverbs 20:3 avoiding strife brings a man honor, but every fool is quarrelsome. Let's cheer each other on even if our buildings have different names, we still are ONE BODY.

KEEP MOVING FORWARD

NOTES: DATE:

_____

_____

_____

_____

_____

_____

_____

_____

_____

_____

_____

_____

The Lord never leaves us

Day 6
Scripture: Psalm 94:18, 19 when I said, "My foot is slipping," "your unfailing love, Lord, supported me. When anxiety was great within me, your consolation brought me joy."

One thing I know to be true in this life is that God will never leave you nor forsake you. Duet 31:8 And the Lord; He is the one who goes before you. He will be with you; He will not leave you nor forsake you; do not fear nor be dismayed.

"The hardest trials of my life was when my son & husband passed away, the people I felt should have been there for me, had all abandoned me, I was left with pain, sorrow, and a lot of unanswered questions to deal with by myself. I felt like I was going to lose my mind. Anxiety would grip me, and I literally had to tell myself to calm down.

Deuteronomy 31:6 be strong and courageous. Do not be afraid or terrified because of them, for the LORD your God goes with you; he will never leave you nor forsake you."

The reason why it feels like God is repeating himself in the scripture, is because the word "forsake "here is translated as I won't "emotionally abandon you." At times when you feel like you can't go on or feel like no one understands your struggle. Remember that you are not alone, God will carry you through the anxiety, the loneliness, the fear, the pain, and the emotional roller coaster life brings your way.

KEEP MOVING FORWARD

NOTES: DATE:

_____

_____

_____

_____

_____

_____

_____

_____

_____

_____

_____

Faithful in someone else's vision

Day 7

Scripture: Luke 16:12 says and if you are not faithful with other people's things (Vision), why should you be trusted with things of your own?

One thing my Pastor always taught us was "faithfulness", not only to God, but to be faithful in every area of our lives. Especially to be faithful in another man's vision.

He knew that at one point in time we would all have our own visions & dreams that we wanted to accomplish in our lives, and we can't do or accomplish any vision without people. We must first be faithful in another man's vision so we can be called trustworthy of our own.

It just saddens my heart to see very few at the days of church clean up. I think we forget that it's not Pastor's church But it's "Gods house" I believe we get so caught up in different feelings and mentalities that we miss the picture and the main point of why we do what we do.

The way you feel shouldn't run your life; this flesh will never 'feel' like doing "nothing."

Everything you do should be because you are "grateful" for what God has and is doing for you, where would you be without Him? ask God to help you to be faithful in the little so He can put you over much.

Luke 16:10 When we bless God's house and His people, God will bless our house and our people.

KEEP MOVING FORWARD

NOTES: DATE:

_____

_____

_____

_____

_____

_____

_____

_____

_____

_____

_____

_____

Listening and doing

Day 8
Scripture: James 1:19 my dear brothers and sisters, take note of this: Everyone should be quick to listen, slow to speak and slow to become angry.

There's a saying 'hurt people will always hurt people' When you listen to those who have hurt you, take a deep look at the root, (hurt) beneath their pain.

Hurt people will always lash out at others, so instead of becoming offended, stop and listen. The Holy Spirit will give you an understanding of why people act and behave the way they do, he'll give you wisdom on how to handle the situation, when you get so upset over the other persons words and behavior, your first natural instinct is to protect yourself.

When you get the understanding, that God is your defender and your shield. You can become a good "listener" and not become angry so quickly. I've had people lash out at me for no reason, but I've learned to "listen" and control my tongue and not join in on the fiasco that the enemy is trying to pull me into.

Everyone even a child can say what's on their mind. But it takes controlled strength to be quiet and listen. Many will see it as weakness, but don't worry about what others think of you.

If you find yourself being opposite of what a child of God should look like its ok, start today by asking God to help you.

KEEP MOVING FORWARD

NOTES: DÀTE:

_____

_____

_____

_____

_____

_____

_____

_____

_____

_____

_____

He is your inheritance

Day 9

Scripture: Psalms 16:5 Lord, you alone are my inheritance, my cup of blessing. You guard all that is mine.

God has left you an inheritance, an inheritance of peace, joy, love, sound mind. But because you don't know, you walk around as an orphan.

God's word says in John 10:10 the thief comes only to steal and kill and destroy. I came that they may have life and have it abundantly He came to give us life here on earth. Many are waiting to get their inheritance when they die. But God wants you to live with abundant life here on earth.

Not only did He leave you with an inheritance of abundant life, but He also wants you to walk as a child of God.

Know who you are, everything belongs to Him & He is your Father, we have not because we ask not.

Stop living a defeated, poor, discouraged life.

Psalms 43:5 why are you discouraged? Why is my heart so sad? I will put my hope In God! I will praise Him again my Savior and my God!

Why are you discouraged? Are you hoping in the wrong things? Hope in Christ because the inheritance He has left for you, will give you everything you need.

KEEP MOVING FORWARD

NOTES: DATE:

_____

_____

_____

_____

_____

_____

_____

_____

_____

_____

_____

_____

Get your affairs in Order

Day 10
Scripture: Duet 6:5 Love the LORD your God with all your heart and with all your soul and with all your strength.

As you can see everything that is going on around you, you can see the coming of the Lord is near. Do not be like the 5 foolish virgins that didn't bring extra oil, they had to go out and look for oil, meanwhile the groom came, and the door was shut and no one else was able to enter. Matt 25:1-13.

When my husband got sick with cancer, he got a phone call from one of the doctors that were attending him and his words were, you are not going to live any longer than 6 months, get all your affairs in order. So that's exactly what we did, God is calling you today giving you a warning, My return is near get all your affairs in order do not take the horrifying acts you see going on around you as something that is just happening, be wise and take heed.

Matthew 24:37-39 for just like the days of Noah were, so the coming of the Son of Man will be. 38 For in those days before the flood, people were eating and drinking, marrying and giving in marriage, until the day Noah entered the ark. 39 And they knew nothing until the flood came and took them all away. It will be the same at the coming of the Son of Man.

I pray you do a self-examination today, and ask God what needs to be put in order in your life, so you could live a life worthy of his calling.

KEEP MOVING FORWARD

NOTES: DATE:

_____

_____

_____

_____

_____

_____

_____

_____

_____

_____

_____

When you speak negative of others.

Day 11
Scripture: James 3:2 if we can control our speech, we can control all areas of our lives.

The next time you feel the urge to trash talk someone whether it's a mean boss at work, a family member you don't agree with, a lazy co-worker, and a sibling you've had a dispute with. Always keep in mind that anyone can throw words around, even a child says things he will regret, but it takes a real strong mature person to keep their mouth away from slander.

Titus 3:1, 2 Christians are told to "speak evil of no one." even when you feel you have the right to speak negative of others, it's not a good choice. It's easy to complain about other people but when we do this, we not only tell our listeners something bad about the person we're talking about.

We also show them our own flaws. Are you gossiping to one friend about another friend who gets under your skin? What you're really doing is telling the one friend that she can't trust you. When you talk about someone's short comings, you're showing your lack of integrity.

If you're wondering why you haven't gotten the promotion it may be because you have allowed strife in your life.

KEEP MOVING FORWARD

NOTES: DATE:

_____

_____

_____

_____

_____

_____

_____

_____

_____

_____

_____

Stay Focused

Day 12

Scripture: Phil 3:13, 14. Brethren, I count not myself to have apprehended: but this one thing I do, forgetting those things which are behind, and reaching forth unto those things which are before, I press on toward the goal for the prize of the upward call of God in Christ Jesus.

In life the enemy comes and brings many challenges many obstacles to try and lure you off course, his focus is to steal your God given purpose. We all want to hear the words "Well done good and faithful servant" and that is why you should do what you do because you're on an assignment from God to fulfill and complete your purpose.

But that gets challenging when the enemy comes to steal your happiness, kill your dreams, and try to destroy your purpose. I've had some very hard challenges in Life when my son died in a car accident & when I had seen my husband Pastor Robert die from Cancer, and I'm pretty sure life hasn't been easy for you at times either.

But God's grace covers you with strength and joy to continue. Remember God sees what you're going through, and his word says he never leaves you nor forsakes you; there is nothing you can't go through because his strength will always be sufficient for you.

So, whatever you may be facing today, keep pushing.

Stay focused! Do not pay any mind to what the enemy throws your way. When your mind is stayed on Jesus, He will give you the strength that you need.

KEEP MOVING FORWARD

NOTES: DATE:

_____

_____

_____

_____

_____

_____

_____

_____

_____

_____

_____

_____

Envy makes the bones rot

Day 13
Scripture: Proverbs 14:30 a tranquil heart gives life to the flesh, but envy makes the bones rot.

When jealousy of others starts to grow in your heart you become unhappy, bitter, and live a life of no peace. Your life becomes a life of competition and you will always want more bigger and better things.

2 Corinth 10:12 we do not dare to classify or compare ourselves with some who commend themselves. When they measure themselves by themselves and compare themselves with themselves, they are NOT WISE.

God has made us all unique in our own way, and no one can beat you, at being you. Jealousy makes you do things to hurt people, and God is not pleased with those actions. Children of God should live a quiet and peaceful life. Do not bring the mentality of the world into your Christian life, it will not only destroy you, but it will also destroy those around you.

Matthew 5:9 blessed is the peacemakers: for they shall be called the children of God.

Walking in God's confidence is to know that God Loves you and God will bless you, and God's grace and favor follows you wherever you go.

KEEP MOVING FORWARD

NOTES: DATE:

_____

_____

_____

_____

_____

_____

_____

_____

_____

_____

_____

_____

KEEP MOVING FORWARD

Seasons come & seasons go

Day 14
God will allow times of separation, so His voice is the only voice you hear.

There will be seasons when it feels like your all alone, seasons of feeling abandoned & rejected. Seasons of feeling mistreated, and abused, seasons of feeling like no one cares.

These are the seasons where God can shape & mold you, the times where His voice becomes louder than the voices that use to control you.

You know those voices, that kept you bound to the old you, to the old ways of thinking, to the old ways of doing things.

God is trying to take you into a new season He hasn't abandoned you. He is taking you to a new land, a land of milk & honey. He's taking you to a land where fruitfulness does exist.

If you can only get pass the feelings & the emotions and look beyond the walls that kept, you bound. You will walk into the Land of more than enough.

Wait on God don't be so in a hurry to come out of this season-being alone with the master gives Him permission to chip away at the dead things and bring new things to life.

You will get over this season, you will live & not die, you will enter the promise land, and you will have more than enough!!!

KEEP MOVING FORWARD

NOTES: DATE:

_____

_____

_____

_____

_____

_____

_____

_____

_____

_____

_____

_____

Never thirst again

Day 15
John 4:14 but whoever drinks the water I give them will never thirst. Indeed, the water I give them will become in them a spring of water welling up to eternal life.

Many are drawn to other things for false comfort; they will find comfort in the wrong people, in various activities, comfort in speaking ill of others, and find comfort in the horoscope.

"When you seek God with ALL you heart and soul, you will come to find that He not only brings true comfort, but He also brings fulfillment in every area that you fill empty. He will fulfill you.

Not things, not people, not various activities, BUT God completes, and satisfies you.

Isaiah 58:11 the Lord will guide you continually and satisfy your desire in scorched (dry) places and make your bones strong; and you shall be like a watered garden, like a spring of water, whose waters do not fail.

So next time you feel alone, discouraged, anxiety, unfilled unsatisfied, go to the Living Source and He will complete you.

Matthew 5:8 "Blessed are those who hunger and thirst for righteousness, for they shall be SATISFIED!!! All these other things come in and will choke Gods word that is within you.

KEEP MOVING FORWARD

NOTES: DATE:

_____

_____

_____

_____

_____

_____

_____

_____

_____

_____

_____

Fear of man

Day 16
Scripture: Proverbs 29:25 Fear of man will prove to be a snare, but whoever trusts in the Lord is kept safe.

At times trusting in the Lord gets pretty hard. We are seeing many people die due to the hurricanes and other disasters all around us.

Whoever trust in the Lord is kept safe, there's another scripture that says "it is impossible to please God without faith. That's why your whole mindset needs to be transformed.

Your old way of thinking needs to be washed by God's word so you can learn to trust in him daily. Not looking at the circumstances that are occurring around you but focusing on His word and His Love for you. We are kept safe, not only by natural disasters but from people who would want to harm you. Psalms 118:6 the LORD is for me, so I will have no fear. What can mere people do to me?

No matter what you see or what you hear. God's promises are true, and you are kept safe under his wings.
Psalms 91:4 He will cover you with his feathers. He will shelter you with his wings. His faithful promises are your armor and protection.

So, no more worrying about your safety no matter who will want to destroy you, God is on your side and that is all you will ever need.

Duet 20:4 for the LORD your God is He that goes with you, to fight for you against your enemies, to save you.

KEEP MOVING FORWARD

NOTES: DATE:

_____

_____

_____

_____

_____

_____

_____

_____

_____

_____

_____

God knows what's best for you

Day 17
Scripture: Proverbs 16:9 a man's heart plans his way, But the Lord directs his steps.

Many times, we wonder how things will turn out. But God is in control of our lives. When you surrendered your life to Christ you were saying, Lord here's my life, do with it what you please, use me as you see fit.

But as time goes by you can forget those words and become selfish with your life and think you know what's best for you.

Proverbs 16:1 to man belong the plans of the heart, but from the Lord comes the reply of the tongue." That's a very powerful statement. God is saying, in effect, "I gave you the vision. Now you put the plan on paper, and I will work out the details."

He's saying he will put everything in order in your life. Let's leave it to God to direct your steps, since he knows what's best for you, he's a good God and will never lead you astray!

You can get used to running your own life that you will make a mess of things and keep going in a big circle.

Gods plan for your life is much better than anything you can put together; as you take one day at a time and stay in his word, he will direct your steps.

His plans for you are better than anything you can ever dream of.

KEEP MOVING FORWARD

NOTES: DATE:

_____

_____

_____

_____

_____

_____

_____

_____

_____

_____

_____

Believing when not seeing

Day 18
Scripture: Hebrews11:1 Faith is the confidence that what we hope for will happen; it gives us assurance about things we cannot see.

Waiting becomes hard at times. But falling away or stepping back from the things we are hoping for, is not an option.

Whether it is your children's salvation, the finances you have been waiting for, or your health to get back to normal. Whatever it may be God's word says in 2Cor 5:7 for we live by believing and not by seeing. That's easier said than done right.

It's hard to believe, especially when you can't see anything manifesting in your life. In fact, your children are still acting a fool, and your heath is escalating, your bills are increasing and the thing you are hoping for isn't coming quick enough.

The enemy will always speak in your ear and say, see I told you God isn't going to do what he said he would do. He will always try and make you quit or distract you with other things, so you can give up and try other methods. He will try to lure you away from receiving your blessing.

I'm telling you today DO NOT GIVE UP. Your blessing, your answered prayer is on its way. Stay true and hold on. God is not a man that should lie, take one day at a time, and continue to believe, even when things become impossible.

Stay focused and do not believe the lie. I am here to remind you that your blessing is on its way.

KEEP MOVING FORWARD

NOTES: DATE:

_____

_____

_____

_____

_____

_____

_____

_____

_____

_____

_____

_____

Vision

Day 19
Scripture: Habakkuk 2:2 And the LORD answered me, and said, write the vision, and make it plain upon tables, that he may run that read it.

First thing you will need to do is - write your vision on paper, then get a scripture to stand on - so when the enemy comes with lies, you will have evidence that this vision will come to pass no matter what it looks like.

When you have a vision – distraction will be your number #1 enemy so do everything in your power to stay focused.

You will not be able to share your vision with everyone because just like Jesus could not perform any miracles in his own town, because the people who knew him had unbelief.

When they would see Jesus, they only saw Him as the carpenter. People will only see you as the old person and will try to talk to out of your vision.

Stay true to your vision God will supply every financial need for your vision to come to pass.

Your vision will need to be bigger than you - If you can make your vision come to pass on your own, then you don't need God & that's an indication that this vision is not of God because God only does BIG things.

Have confidence to know that it won't be you fulfilling this God given dream, but it will be God using you to make this happen.

Don't settle for anything less, than what He showed you.

KEEP MOVING FORWARD

NOTES: DATE:

_____

_____

_____

_____

_____

_____

_____

_____

_____

_____

_____

_____

Memories of your past

Day 20
Scripture: Philippians 3:13 Many times when you are trying to get ahead-here comes the enemy always trying to show you your past mistakes, your bad decisions, and your failures, your lack of achievements.

I will not be held to the memory of my past while God is trying to show me my future.

I don't know what your past may look like BUT I do know that God is more interested in your future.

He has good things in store for you, the bible says in Jeremiah 29:11 that He has plans for you, plans to prosper you, to give you a hope and a future.

Stop looking backwards, stop putting yourself down, stop believing the lie that you will never amount to much, that you're never going to make it, that your life is worth nothing.

And start believing that God has made a way where there is no way, that Gods favor is on your life, that His mercies are renewed daily, that his healing power is greater.

When the enemy tries to remind you of your past failures remind him of his future.

There is nothing but good things up ahead for you-stay focused and don't doubt the goodness of God.

He is faithful to His word & His promises.

KEEP MOVING FORWARD

NOTES: DATE:

_____

_____

_____

_____

_____

_____

_____

_____

_____

_____

_____

He'll draw you out

Day 21
Scripture: Psalm 18:16-17 He reached down from on high and took hold of me; he drew me out of deep waters. He rescued me from my powerful enemy.

No matter what difficulty you may be facing, God has a plan to draw you out, you may feel overwhelmed, but know that God is reaching out His hand to you.

He won't let you sink, and He won't let you slip. He'll take hold of you and rescue you from the deep waters of opposition that rage against you.

If you are facing adversity, know that you are not facing it alone. God is with you, and He is for you.

Sometimes there are trials you will go through where it will seem like there is nothing no one can do to help you.

You will feel so overwhelmed that you will not want to get out of bed and depression will hit you so hard that all your strength will be gone.

The desire for life & the desire to do anything is taken away. When this happens, you will have to look to God for strength and power.

You will have to force yourself to not allow the enemy to win this battle.

I say that today – you will be stronger than your struggle!! You will win today because it's through His strength that you have overcome!!!

KEEP MOVING FORWARD

NOTES: DATE:

_____

_____

_____

_____

_____

_____

_____

_____

_____

_____

_____

_____

KEEP MOVING FORWARD

Don't look back

Day 22
Scripture: Genesis 19:17, 26 so it came to pass, when they had brought them outside, that he said, "Escape for your life! Do not look behind you nor stay anywhere in the plain. Escape to the mountains, lest you be destroyed." vs. 26 But his wife looked back behind him, and she became a pillar of salt.

What made Lot's wife look back? What was she tied to in her soul that she felt like she just had to look back? The angels of the Lord gave Lot and his family clear directions as they were escaping the destruction in Sodom and Gomorrah.

They specifically told them, "Don't look back. Behind them was an old way of life, a city filled with idolatry, lust, sin, and many other things that were against God. Because Lot was Abraham's nephew, and God had a covenant with Abraham, he and his family were being spared from the destruction of the city.

Many things may try to pull you back to your old lifestyle or your old ways, the familiar spirits will come back to see if you have really changed, if you have really made that commitment to move forward.

You need to understand that God is saying to you today.

"Don't look back; I'm bringing you into a new place, with a new future." A future filled with new promises and new blessings.

Just stay focused on what is ahead. I will show you a new thing that you know not of.

50

KEEP MOVING FORWARD

NOTES: DATE:

_____

_____

_____

_____

_____

_____

_____

_____

_____

_____

_____

Doing things unto the father

Day 23

Scripture: Colossians 3:17 And whatever you do in word or deed, do all in the name of the Lord Jesus, giving thanks to God the Father through Him.

I remember when I first got saved I was more than happy to do everything and anything the Pastors or leaders, would have us do, I didn't care who got the credit I didn't care if anyone noticed, I was just so excited to be used by God.

But as time went by, I started noticing that I was the only one picking up the papers, or even noticed negative remarks about how others didn't want to attend certain functions, then I even heard that a sister was spreading lies about me, when in fact all I did was LOVE that sister, and pour endless hours of time encouraging her to not give up.

I was so discouraged on how someone could repay me with evil. Then one day God spoke to me and said Maribel if you're doing things expecting to get noticed, or expecting people to bless you in return, then that's all you're going to get.

You will get a pat on the back a thank you and even have lies spread about you.

"But when you do things unto God, He will repay you. God will make sure all your needs are met. He will expose all lies & guard you from your enemy.

KEEP MOVING FORWARD

NOTES: DATE:

_____

_____

_____

_____

_____

_____

_____

_____

_____

_____

_____

_____

A religious Spirit

Day 24
Scripture: But the Lord said to Samuel, "Do not look at his appearance or at his physical stature, because I have refused him. For the Lord does not see as man sees; for man looks at the outward appearance, but the Lord looks at the heart." 1 Samuel 16:7

Sometimes like the Pharisees we can also get to caught up in the outer appearance of man, rather than seeing what God is doing on the inside of them.

 I don't believe God is too much interested in what we are wearing, yes women shouldn't wear skirts that show more than normal, and yes women shouldn't be showing all there women parts, But when it becomes the focus in your life and heart you become like the Pharisees very judgmental.

I believe God has made us all unique and we all have our own style, if someone isn't dressed like you or looks like you, don't become so judgmental that you view a person with your religious standards.

Don't become so focused on the outer appearance that you miss what God is trying to do in their lives.

Luke 11:38, 39 But the Pharisee was surprised when he noticed that Jesus did not first wash before the meal. Then the Lord said to him, "Now then, you Pharisees clean the outside of the cup and dish, but inside you are full of greed and wickedness. If you have been judging others by their appearance let's change it today ask God to give you a heart to receive others just the way they are, not the way you think they should be.

KEEP MOVING FORWARD

NOTES: DATE:

_____

_____

_____

_____

_____

_____

_____

_____

_____

_____

_____

No one is perfect

Day 25
Scripture: Romans 8:1, 2 Therefore, there is now no condemnation for those who are in Christ Jesus, because through Christ Jesus the law of the Spirit of life set me free from the law of sin and death.

When I was in the women's home it was easy to serve God. They told us when to pray, when to read, I felt so clean from all impurities of this world. (Perfect).

But when I went home, I had no one telling me what to do. When I wouldn't pray for one day, I felt like I had to start all over again, I felt like I had sinned.

I thought I had to be perfect, it was crazy to have thought that Way. The enemy would always bring condemnation and I would feel bad.

I would always wonder how Christians could live a sinless life, I would think man I don't think I can do this, this is too hard for me, I wanted to serve God, but in my mind it was so hard for me to be perfect.

Romans 3:23 says - so we are all sinners, and all fall short of his glory. God expects us to make mistakes because we are still in this humanly body. No one is perfect but Christ. We will all make mistakes, but it's important that we learn from them and get back up and continue our journey in Christ.

Don't allow the enemy to bring condemnation and keep you down. Get back up today and shake it off, and with God's help and his strength, you can be stronger than ever.

KEEP MOVING FORWARD

NOTES: DATE:

_____

_____

_____

_____

_____

_____

_____

_____

_____

_____

_____

Finishing strong

Day 26

Scripture: Hebrews 10:25 says not forsaking our meeting together [as believers for worship and instruction], as is the habit of some, but encouraging one another; and all the more [faithfully] as you see the day [of Christ's return] approaching.

Many are giving up on church and people. I've heard some say, I can watch the preacher from home, and I don't need to go to church.

Yes, true but God's word also says in Proverbs 27:17 as iron sharpens iron, so one person sharpens another. We grow by sharpening each other we cannot come to the maturity of Christ and do what God has called us to do by staying home.

God has called us as one body and we need each other to grow and survive. I understand that we all get hurt by church members, pastors, family, ect. But we need to stay focused and faithful to God and continue to grow together in church, and encourage one another, loving one another, exhorting one another.

There's a reason why God added this scripture to his word, he knew that there is strength in numbers; he knew that the enemy would try and isolate us and keep us away from Gods word and God's people.

1 Timothy 4:1 now the Spirit explicitly says that in the later times some will desert the faith and occupy themselves with deceiving spirits and demonic teachings.

Don't desert the teachings that you've been taught, stay faithful and committed until the end.

KEEP MOVING FORWARD

NOTES: DATE:

_____

_____

_____

_____

_____

_____

_____

_____

_____

_____

_____

You're on a mission

Day 27

You don't have time to waste-souls are dying, marriages are broken, relationships are hurting, people are injured and sick.

I come to find out that people will love you, until they don't need you anymore.

People will follow you until you say something that hurts their ego, People will love you until you surpass them.

We all have been given an assignment and in order to fulfill that call on your life-you are going to have to stay focused.

Pay no mind to who doesn't like you and who talks about you. You are called to win souls not to make it into any popularity contest.

Love those who hate you, love those who persecute you, pray for those who talk bad about you. You're going to have to have thick skin in order to make it.

If no one cheers you on, cheer yourself on, if no one likes your post like your own post.

Retrain your mind today & say - I feel good because Jesus loves me and He accepts me, He has called me His own.

And because of that- I can walk in the confidence to know that I am worth dying for.

'I AM WORTH EVERYTHING HE HAS FOR ME"

KEEP MOVING FORWARD

NOTES: DATE:

_____

_____

_____

_____

_____

_____

_____

_____

_____

_____

_____

Conditioned to blame others

Day 28
When things are not going as they should be, or when the outcome didn't come out as you expected, maybe it's time to look with-in.

I remember when I was using drugs; I always used that excuse "well my dad was an alcoholic so that's why I am a drug addict.' In some cases, it's true because curses are passed down from generations BUT it was my choice to be in the condition that I found myself in.

It's much easier to shift the blame on others than to look with-in. It's my parents' fault, it's my bosses fault, and it's my kids fault, it's everyone else's fault.

I know it's a hard thing to do because now you are taking the blame for your life & taking responsibility for your situation rather than pointing fingers.

But then and only then can God come in and help you, now you are allowing him to show you what you must do to make your situation better.

Proverbs 28:13 whoever conceals his transgression (wrongs) will not prosper, but he who confesses and forsakes them will obtain mercy.

Take responsibility for your life today, and once you do that, you will see that God is allowed free access to come in and turn things around and make life so much better.

KEEP MOVING FORWARD

NOTES: DATE:

_____

_____

_____

_____

_____

_____

_____

_____

_____

_____

God's unmerited favor

Day 29
Scripture: Genesis 39:21 But the Lord was with Joseph
and extended kindness to him and gave him favor in the
sight of the chief jailer.

God's favor follows you wherever you go, he opens doors
that no man can shut, and he makes a way where there is
no way. Isaiah 43:19 See I am doing a new thing! Now it
shall spring, up; do you not perceive it? I am making a way
in the wilderness and streams in the wasteland.

A dessert is a dry place where nothing exists here God is
saying even if you don't know anybody, even if you're not
qualified for the job, even if you don't have the finances for
it, even if your body is yelling at you saying you're not
going to make it, even if they lied about you God is the one
leading you and opening those doors of financial
breakthroughs, of healing, of a better job, of your purpose
coming to pass.

You see even if you were in the dessert where no one or
nothing was around, God's favor follows you, and He will
open doors, He will make it happen, He will bring divine
connections because God is orchestrating your life.

God will make it happen for you. No need to be begging,
no need to be kissing butt, no need to try and make it
happen, no need to put others down to make yourself look
better, no need to lie and cheat.

There's no need for all of that. Why? Because Gods favor
is on you and follows you wherever you go. And he will
make it come to pass.

KEEP MOVING FORWARD

NOTES: DATE:

A jezebel spirit

Day 30

If you are not familiar with these types of people you can easily get caught in their web of manipulation.

It is very difficult to escape their lies because they repeatedly tell you that if you leave, you're not going to make it, or you will fall without their leadership or their relationship.

Narcissist will always have the need to impress others, which will cause them to stretch the truth about their lives.

They require constant praise and feel superior to others. They take advantage of others, and have no sympathy when others are in need.

If you find that this is, you or that you are caught in a web of a narcissist and can't break free. Don't lose hope the same way God helped me get out of this web He can deliver you.

It took me awhile to be free from the mind control and manipulation of a narcissist, but I am thinking for myself now and have the confidence that the narcissist took from me.

God always answers our prayers He will not leave you or abandon you. He gives strength to the weary and boldness to those that need it.

Ask God to deliver you today and bring you a step closer to your healing and deliverance In Jesus name.

KEEP MOVING FORWARD

NOTES: DATE:

_____

_____

_____

_____

_____

_____

_____

_____

_____

_____

_____

KEEP MOVING FORWARD

SCRIPTURES TO STAND ON WHILE MOVING FORWARD!

Isaiah 55:11 so shall my word be that goeth forth out of my mouth: it shall not return unto me void, but it shall accomplish that which I please, and it shall prosper in the thing whereto I sent it.

Romans 10:17 so then faith cometh by hearing, and hearing by the word of God.

2 Timothy 1:7 for God has not given us a spirit of fear, but of power and of love and of a sound mind.

Philippians 3:13-14 Brethren, I count not myself to have apprehended: but this one thing I do, forgetting those things which are behind, and reaching forth unto those things which are before, [14] I press toward the mark for the prize of the high calling of God in Christ Jesus.

Deuteronomy 31:6 _Be strong and of a good courage, fear not, nor be afraid of them: for the LORD thy God, he it is that doth go with thee; he will not fail thee, nor forsake thee.

Exodus 23:25 "So you shall serve the LORD your God, and He will bless your bread and your water. And I will take sickness away from the midst of you."

Matthew 22:37 Jesus said unto him, Thou shalt love the Lord thy God with all thy heart, and with all thy soul, and with all thy mind.

KEEP MOVING FORWARD

Made in the
USA
Lexington, KY